PANDORA'S BOX IS OPEN

NOW WHAT DO I DO?

A PARENT'S GUIDE
FOR HELPING
CHILDREN WHO
HAVE BEEN EXPOSED
TO PORNOGRAPHY

D1605103

BY GAIL POYNER, PH.D., LICENSED PSYCHOLOGIST

Beacon House Press
www.closingpandorasbox.com
www.facebook.com/closingpandorasbox

BEACON
HOUSE PRESS

For information about special discounts available for bulk purchases or
sales, contact the author at drpoyner@sbcglobal.net.
Graphic Design by Christine Poyner

To the loves of my life, my husband Gene,
my six children and those who call me Granny.

Table of Contents

Gail Poyner

Dr. Gail Poyner is a Licensed Psychologist in private practice in Oklahoma. After raising six children, she returned to school and received her doctorate in psychology. Over the past sixteen years of counseling adults, teens and children, she has become increasingly disturbed by the ever escalating number of teens and children who have become addicted to pornography.

For years, Dr. Poyner has treated adults struggling with pornography addiction, but when she was confronted with the astonishing number of children and teens addicted to pornography, she began looking for resources to treat them as well. Unfortunately, she found none.

Parents around the nation have contacted Dr. Poyner asking what they can do to help their children with the issue of pornography addiction. Many have been desperate to find a therapist who treats this problem but, almost universally, they say they have met with little success. This book was written to fill that gap—both for parents and treating professionals.

What you will read took three years of research to write. Dr. Poyner has combined her experience, expertise and extensive knowledge about the biological, cognitive and behavioral aspects of pornography addiction with psychological principles known to promote behavior change in children and teenagers.

Dr. Poyner engages in public presentations on the issue of childhood pornography addiction and the importance of teaching children skills they need when, not if, they are confronted with pornography. Dr. Poyner is also a strong advocate of prevention and educating parents about how to preclude, as much as possible, child and teen access to pornography.

"Computers have emerged as the leading-edge technology for the distribution of pornography."
– Donna Rice Hughes

CHAPTER ONE

The Truth is Out: *Your Child Has Been Exposed to Pornography*

Your Child Has Been Exposed To Pornography

If you are reading this book it is probably because you are either concerned that your child or adolescent may have been exposed to pornography, or you have discovered that it has already happened. The parents I have talked to say that when they discover their child's porn use, they experience a wide range of distressing emotional reactions. That is perfectly normal and you are not alone.

Most parents want to keep their children away from pornography, but the fact is that an alarming number of kids are already actively viewing it. The type and extent of the exposure or use may vary, but when parents discover that Pandora's Box is already open, and that one of its most troubling problems has escaped, most don't know what to do. That is why I wrote this book.

Some parents think that once a child has been into porn, there is no going back. Maybe that is how you are feeling. However, helping your child stay away from pornography—even when they've already been exposed—is not a hopeless endeavor. The good news is that you can teach your child that pornography can quickly become an addiction and that pornography can harm them. Equally important is that you can teach them skills to manage the feelings that accompany a strong attraction to this dangerous material.

Pornography is Pervasive, Powerful, and Harmful to Children

Accessing today's pornography is incredibly simple. Pornography is a multi-billion-dollar industry. Its success is due, in large part, to the social Internet's ability to make pornography available to anyone anywhere, even when we don't go looking for it. And just like a drug, its ability to draw people into addiction is incredibly powerful—especially when its consumers are young.

Some people don't believe that pornography is a problem, but parents need to know that its use can have lasting neurological and behavioral repercussions that you and your child may not know about. Understanding the importance of the biological components of a pornography addiction represents the first step toward helping your child find freedom from pornography.

What You Will Learn in This Book

You might not think you have what it takes to help your child learn to break free of pornography. However, you have spent years teaching and influencing your child and this situation is no different. You can help them resist pornography with strength and resolve.

You taught your child to wear a seat belt, to be cautious about strangers and what to do in the event of a house fire. In each of these cases, you likely taught your child two things. First, you taught them why certain things are dangerous. Second, you taught them what to do to keep them safe. Knowledge first and behavior second. Parents can use those same principles to help a child who is using pornography. This book will give you and your child information and tools to learn together and then teach you how to take action.

Making the case for teaching safety is probably an easy sell. But what about trying to influence a child to stop a behavior, such as pornography use? What about when the behavior has become addictive? This book is designed to help you help your child with that very problem. You might ask why I believe I can help parents and children with pornography addiction.

About fifteen years ago, I began seeing a few men who had an addiction to pornography. Over the years, however, the number of men who struggle with this problem has increased exponentially. Now, the floodgates of Internet porn are open and an ocean of the vilest and most perverse media has flooded the earth, with absolutely no governmental intervention.

With few exceptions, the men I treat for this problem are depressed, and it's the same for many children. For men who are married, virtually every one of them reports high levels of marital distress, which they say is directly related to their addiction to pornography.

Here is the good news: Many of the men I have treated have gone on to master their pornography addiction. It takes a lot of hard work, but I have seen it happen. So how does that apply to children?

Parents across the nation have contacted me asking for names of mental health professionals who are known to treat children for problems related to pornography use. Unfortunately, other than in one or two states, I haven't been able to locate a therapist who treats this type of problem in children and adolescents. To fill that gap, I decided to write this book. It has taken over three years to develop the methods you will find in this book. I took sound psychological principles central to promoting behavior change in children and adolescents, and combined them with what we know about child development and what biological forces influence their behavior.

I went on to extensively research how pornography interacts with a child's brain, then linked my research with what I have found to be effective in helping both adults and children free themselves from the riptide of pornography addiction.

I will admit that it's a struggle for children and adolescents to manage a pornography addiction. One of the biggest reasons is living in a sexualized society where pornography is so easy to access. Remember, helping your child master a pornography addiction is a process, not an event. You will need to use the skills you learn in this book over and over again.

I know that parents can become educated parents who go on to teach and support their children in successfully freeing themselves from the quicksand of pornography's pull. Again, it's not necessarily easy, but it can be done.

Don't forget: You play a very powerful role in your child's life. My goal is to help you harness and use the power of knowledge, relationship, love, and skill. In these pages, you will learn how to use my five-step plan, which includes how to:

1. *Manage your Emotions*

2. *Identify your Goal*

3. *Become Educated*

4. *Educate and Teach Skills*

5. *Develop a Plan and Act on it*

Before we talk about the five-step plan, let's talk about Pandora and her box of trouble. This is important because even though your child may have been exposed to some of the vilest media imaginable, Pandora's story teaches us that there really is hope for recovery.

Pandora and Her Curiosity

In the tradition of Greek mythology, there were two brothers, Prometheus and Epimetheus. Prometheus angered Zeus by stealing fire from him to give to man. The vengeful Zeus, god of sky, lightning, and thunder, ordered Pandora's creation as a blight against mankind for this betrayal. She was the first woman on the earth, and was bestowed with many gifts from the gods, including beauty and curiosity.

Zeus duly punished Prometheus by chaining him to a rock, but his hunger for revenge remained. Zeus next offered Pandora to Prometheus' brother, Epimetheus, to be his wife. Prometheus tried to warn his brother about the dangers of accepting a gift from Zeus, but Epimetheus was so taken with Pandora's beauty, he married her anyway.

Zeus was very clever, so to get back at Prometheus, Zeus gave Pandora what she thought was a wedding gift—a beautiful and very enticing box. No one but Zeus knew that hidden in the box was tragedy, darkness, illness, and hardship. But that wasn't all. To make the box even more enticing, Zeus told Pandora never to open it.

We all know what happened next. Pandora didn't know that her curiosity had the power to change her mythological world. Innocent and naïve about what the box contained, Pandora opened it, only to set free a host of unimaginable evils that instantly spread across the earth.

Every kind of wickedness escaped. One can only imagine Pandora's horror at what she had done. Zeus, however, wasn't troubled at all. This was what he had planned all along. But he was unaware of one important thing. Not all of what was in the box was wicked. Deep in the dark recesses of that beautiful vessel and among the spirits that were released, was Hope.

Much like Pandora, your child is not to blame for stumbling upon pornography, whether intentionally or unintentionally. Sexual development and curiosity are natural. The Internet as a whole, with its many benefits, is not something we can or should avoid.

Pornography is the culprit, and it undermines the use of the Internet as a means to obtain otherwise useful and beneficial information. It's the purveyors of porn who take strategic steps to hide their materials in a box that takes very little effort to open. However, this book has the potential to empower you and your child to stop pornography's perverse pull into addiction.

Armed with hope, your job now is to step bravely into a world in which Pandora's Box is open, and your goal is to teach your child how to control the impulse to view pornography, *before* it controls them.

"Our society is being deluged with sexually explicit displays of beatings, torture, rape, and child abuse as forms of Internet 'entertainment,' with the message that sexual violence is comical and routine."
– Children's Online Safety Act ("COSA") Petition

CHAPTER TWO

The New Box:
How Internet Pornography Entices Our Kids

The Modern Box

Following a hearing in 1996, the U.S. Department of Justice concluded that "Never before in the history of telecommunications media in the United States has so much indecent and obscene material been so easily accessible by so many minors in so many American homes with so few restrictions." Keep in mind that this was *two decades ago*. Since that time pornography has only further saturated the Internet and has become more deviant and more easily accessed by children.

Consider for a moment what pornography was like in the past, and what it's like now. Gone are the days when access to pornography required visiting an "adult" bookstore, or sending away for it. Back then, a "dirty" magazine arrived, as promised, in a plain brown envelope with no return address. Back then, porn was much harder to get. It took effort and in-

cluded the risk of exposure. It wasn't anonymous.

Now, pornography is simply a mouse click or screen tap away. It is completely anonymous and available to anyone of any age, at any time, with little risk of being caught.

In a 2008 Statement to Congress on Pornography, Jeffrey Satinover, MS, MD from Princeton University said of pornography:

"With the advent of the computer, the delivery system for this addictive stimulus has become nearly resistance-free. It is as though we have devised a form of heroin 100 times more powerful than before, usable in the privacy of one's own home and injected directly to the brain through the eyes.

It is now available in unlimited supply via a self-replicating distribution network, glorified as art and protected by the Constitution. And it's not just naked people anymore. Today's pornography is unimaginably perverse, violent, degrading and even inhumane."

Although Pandora and her box were born of Greek mythology, the underlying story is eerily similar to the situation in which we find ourselves now. Our boxes are rectangular, run on electricity and batteries, and although they offer a wealth of good information, they can also be vessels of dangerous material.

What seemingly innocent and enticing boxes are our children exposed to? As much as we like to think we are in control of what they see on the Internet, it's virtually impossible to protect our children at all times. When it comes to pornography, exposure can come from Internet-enabled phones, tablets, computers, television, DVD's, music, books, and movies.

Think about the "gifts" we give our children. Think about a child's natural curiosity. As parents, we may be unintentionally giving them a well-disguised time bomb, ready to go off as soon as the gift is opened. Think about what might be in your child's own box, or those of their friends, the homes of relatives or family friends, schools and libraries. Pornography is there, at all times and in all places, for innocent children to find.

This is the world in which our children live. The Internet represents a modern-day Pandora's Box. If that's not scary enough, consider this: In the past, the porn industry did not target children.

Now, they do.

The Porn Industry is Pandering to Our Youth

The pornography industry is like Zeus. Its purveyors are deliberate in unleashing its addictive power, thereby creating what they believe will be customers for life. They target children, whose curiosity is powerful but also whose awareness of what is harmful is dangerously undeveloped. Once exposed, addiction can come on swift and strong. The porn industry knows that, so they have developed a variety of ways to trap our youth.

Due to deliberately manipulative marketing on the part of the pornography industry, something as simple as misspelling a word in a search engine can result in pages of graphic pornographic sites and images. They do this by having distribution sites purchase URLs and domain names that are similar to popular and legitimate sites, so that even the tiniest spelling error can be turned into a direct path to pornography.

Often, the words they target are those associated with movies or characters commonly searched by children. Similarly, pornographers often sexualize popular cartoon characters and incorporate free and highly enticing games into their interactive websites. Once exposed to a site, distributors employ other tactics, such as pop-up ad bombardment, to reinforce the attraction to pornographic images, as well as to keep its young visitors returning.

Other times, children deliberately seek out this material. The increased availability of pornography goes hand in hand with an ever more sexualized society. A child's natural curiosity may lead them to seek out pornography in order to better understand or experience the overly sexualized things they are exposed to every day in our culture. Heightened awareness comes with heightened curiosity.

Very often, our children are innocently introduced to pornography by their friends, in their own homes, at school, in a relative's home, or at some other place where they are spending time without adult supervision. Some adults may not have restrictions on this type of media because they consider it innocent or a response to natural curiosity. Others may deliberately expose a child to pornography for their own purposes, sometimes with devastating consequences.

Some parents believe that exposure to pornography typically occurs on their home computers, and further believe that putting filters and blocking programs on these devices is sufficient to prevent access to porn. However, research increasingly shows that the majority of pornography children and teenagers are viewing comes from their hand-held devices. Phones and tablets are a mobile, private, and easily accessible

...pornographers often misuse popular cartoon characters and incorporate free flash games that may be attractive to children on their interactive websites.

link to limitless pornography.

Consider a case from my clinical practice. Although the child's name and any potentially identifiable details have been changed, the following illustrates the reality of innocent exposure:

Irvin, an eight-year-old boy, was invited to spend two weeks with his aunt and uncle in another state. Although it would be the first time he would travel by airplane, he was so excited about the trip that he experienced only minor anxiety on take-off. His aunt and uncle had a pool and they lived only a short distance from a lake where they would go boating. Irvin could not have been happier.

One night, Irvin's aunt and uncle went to bed early. The three of them had been at the lake all day and the adults were tired. Being a typical kid, Irvin wanted to stay up and watch TV, so his aunt said he could camp out on the couch. Although she told Irvin it was lights out at 9:30, with no children of her own, she didn't think about pa-

rental controls and the fact that her nephew could access inappropriate material on their cable television.

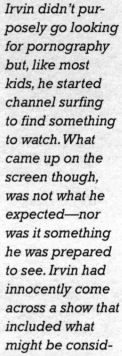

Irvin didn't purposely go looking for pornography but, like most kids, he started channel surfing to find something to watch. What came up on the screen though, was not what he expected—nor was it something he was prepared to see. Irvin had innocently come across a show that included what might be considered mild female nudity. However, it was that nudity and the context of the show's setting that sparked his desire to see more. The fact that Irvin was alone and because of the chemical stimulus released in his brain by the images, the whole incident carried an aura of attraction, intrigue, and mystery.

In the days that followed, the images and sexual situations Irvin had seen, as well as their corresponding feelings of excitement, made finding pornography very enticing. When he returned home, he got onto his family's computer and began looking for pictures of naked women, much like he had seen at his aunt and uncle's house.

However, with the assistance of the pornography industry, an eight-year-old's curiosity and a developmental lack of restraint, in a matter of weeks, Irvin graduated to viewing some of the most disturbing pornography available. In the span of only a few weeks, Irvin developed an incredibly strong addiction to pornography.

With the push of a button, what may seem enticing and exciting can actually cause great harm and have far-reaching consequences for today's youth. Internet-capable phones and tablets are the primary culprits, but as in the case of Irvin, accessing pornographic material can come from boxes that have been in our homes for generations.

Like Zeus's gift, our modern-day boxes are very inviting and have the potential to awaken a type of naïve curiosity similar to Pandora's. However, there is a clear difference between Pandora's mythical box and those of today. We know what's in ours, and we know that when an ever-increasing number of children are exposed to their degrading contents, devastating addictions can follow. Armed with this knowledge, we can fight back.

As we've learned from Pandora's

story, there is hope. Parental influence is essential in not only proactively guarding against pornography use, but in dealing with the repercussions that can follow once a child has been exposed to it.

According to social research, healthy parent-child relationships have the potential to positively impact the value your child places on your participation in helping free them from porn addiction. Even if there are difficulties in the parent-child relationship, the thoughtful and well-planned responses you will be learning in this book can still have a powerful impact on your child's behavior.

Later in this book, I will give you empowering and practical steps to follow so that you can be a positive force in your child's battle against pornography. But first, let's take a look at the damaging effects we are fighting against.

"History has shown us that it can
take years and even generations
before a society understands the
effects of addictive substances."
– Fight the New Drug

CHAPTER THREE

The Invisible Enemy:
How Pornography Can Affect Your Child

We now know that pornography addiction is as real as any other form of addiction. Children at formative ages are especially susceptible to its damaging effects. Their first exposure to pornography releases unnaturally high levels of pleasurable chemicals in the brain. The body grows used to this natural chemical concoction and continues to seek it out. Repeated porn usage delivers this gratifying chemical hit, time after time. Like a drug, kids keep coming back for more, sometimes in response to boredom, but very often as a way to cope with the difficulties and uncertainties of life, which—let's face it— will always exist.

As a result, instead of developing healthy coping techniques, children are becoming tethered at young ages to one of the unhealthiest coping strategies there is: addiction. The porn industry knows this and that's why they want to hook our children while they are young. And they will stop at virtually nothing to do this.

They want customers for life. What better way than to target innocent children who lack the judgment to avoid pornography's perverse pull? So let's look at where that pull can lead our children.

The Realities of Childhood Pornography Addiction

Before we look at how you can help your child with the detrimental effects of pornography, it's important to understand what we're battling and why. Taking a stand against youth and adolescent pornography use is not simply a moral issue, as some may believe, but a physical and emotional one. The truth is, addiction can be severely detrimental to your child's lifelong growth and development. This can result in behavioral, neurological, relationship, and social limitations.

According to Dr. Kevin B. Skinner, a renowned therapist and author who focuses on the treatment of pornography addiction, "The earlier the exposure to pornography, the deeper the client's level of addiction." The reason pornography addiction can easily begin at a young age is because this is when youths are most curious, vulnerable, and impressionable. Sexual development occurs naturally, but when pornography is introduced during such a crucial stage of development, it's like throwing a monkey wrench into a complex arrangement of cogs and wheels. It can alter not only sexual development, but many other aspects of a child's overall functioning.

Pornography Addiction Can Alter the Brain

Addiction, no matter what the substance, is a scientific phenomenon. In this case, your child's brain can actually change as a result of progressive exposure to pornography. According to research conducted by neurosurgeon Dr. Donald L. Hilton, pornography can have long-term and adverse effects on brain structure and functioning. In fact, his research points to evidence that pornography consumption reduces both brain size and brain activity.

Other researchers, such as Dr. Julie Kauer and Dr. Robert Malenka, found that chemical alterations in the brain, such as those caused by pornography consumption, have the potential to severely impact a child's emotions, memories, and overall sense of reality. They discovered that the act of viewing porn stimulates the pleasure response in the brain, which causes the viewer to bond with the stimulant. This means that children who consume porn can form emotional attachments to this dangerous drug, oftentimes using it later in life to replace emotional connections with their sexual partners.

What we can see from this is that the damaging effects of pornography can be both widespread and long-term, which means that many youths not only grow up bound to the effects of pornography addiction, but may never know or understand the many ways in which it is negatively impacting their lives.

Pornography Use Can Cause Behavioral Changes

We know that pornography addiction can affect a child's natural sexual development, but in what ways? One of the most noticeable is their outward behavior. Pornography consumption reinforces notions of sexism and models unhealthy relationships. It supports unrealistic expectations and attitudes of sexual coercion that some children may be tempted to act out in real life.

There are so many ways in which modern adolescents are expressing unhealthy attitudes toward sex. Some of the most prevalent expressions of sexually desensitized youth we see today are sexting, taking and sending overly sexualized photos, having erotic social media conversations, and engaging in sexual experiences at a young age. It is disturbing to realize that a generation of children who have been exposed to the Internet's abundance of pornographic images and sexualized media, can also be a generation of youth who believe that this type of objectification is acceptable.

Children model behaviors, and their perceptions are developed by what they see and experience. What this boils down to is that repeated pornography consumption can shape your child's values and attitudes about sex. A diminished regard for the sexual act and unhealthy beliefs about intimacy have the real possibility of negatively impacting future relationships. Most of the men I treat for pornography addiction say they don't feel as close to their spouses and have less satisfaction in their marriages. The spouses of these men universally say that they feel diminished as women, lack trust in their husbands and worry that the addiction will continue.

A very alarming fact related to pornography consumption is that it puts children at greater risk of sexual exploitation. In the hands of vulnerable children, the Internet can provide a steady diet of perverse media that can easily draw them into a vortex of risk. This is because the porn industry doesn't just give. It takes. As we talked about earlier, too many of our youth are having conversations with, and sending sexual pictures of themselves, to deviant adults posing as young people. Worse yet, these predators are very skilled at offering a counterfeit sense of acceptance, nurturance, and a listening ear, all the while attempting to reel children into face-to-face meetings—sometimes with tragic results.

We must protect our children from online predators and sexual deviants who wish to harm them, and that starts with stopping access to pornography. But we can arm our young ones with the skills they need to avoid the many dangers associated with pornography exposure.

The Addiction Cycle

You've been given a lot of heavy information in this chapter. But there is still no need to fear the worst. The fact that you are reading this shows that you are willing to do what it takes to prevent the scenarios above from becoming a reality for your child.

Before we can move forward, it's important to understand how the progression of a pornography addiction takes place:

1. Attachment This begins during the first contact with pornography. The brain registers a pleasurable chemical response and the mind and body are attracted to these feelings and their associated images. Pretty soon that feel-good chemical gets attached to viewing porn.

2. Escalation Because of the body's physical attraction to pornographic material and the brain's chemical response, children, without the ability to see its danger, want to experience more of it in order to repeatedly access this pleasurable sensation.

3. Desensitization This occurs in conjunction with a continuous escalation of porn consumption. The gratification once delivered by certain types of pornography is no longer achieved, and more extreme pornography must be accessed in order to deliver the same pleasurable response.

4. Addiction Once the pornography addict is desensitized to the material available to them, interpersonal relationships suffer, they see themselves and others differently, isolation often occurs or increases, and they may even begin modeling behaviors they see in pornography. At this point, their behavior is no longer a choice, but a part of their emotional and behavioral system.

This makes sense to us, but it may be a bit much for a child or teen to absorb as it relates to them. Your role in preventing the addiction cycle is critical, and it is important that the cycle of addiction be explained in a manner that your child can understand. In doing this, it's best to use examples your child can identify with. Here are a few examples you may choose to use in talking with your child:

This first example is for a younger child:

Set the scene: Let's say a kid gets a new bicycle.

Explain the attachment: The first thing he wants to do is get outside and ride the new bike. Riding up and down the street makes him feel good.

Demonstrate the escalation: **Now, let's say that the kid gets tired of riding up and down the street, so he decides to go down a small hill. That's even more fun, so he pushes the bike up one of the biggest hills in the neighborhood, and even though it's dangerous, he loves the excitement and he doesn't recognize that what he is doing may cause harm to himself.**

Show the addiction: **Because the big hill is really, really exciting, the boy doesn't go back to smaller hills because they aren't as exciting** as the big hill. Soon, he might not want to ride his bike at all if he can't ride down bigger and bigger hills. Now, what if he decides that riding up and down the hill is better than playing with friends? Let's say that he ends up getting a better bike and all he can think about is doing dangerous tricks. What might happen if all a kid wants to do is ride a bike? He might lose friends who have other interests. He probably won't find out about other fun things to do, or that he may be good at them and enjoy them. And because he doesn't recognize that what he's doing is dangerous, he may end up getting hurt.

Give hope for recovery: **The good news is that the boy can turn to other things to help him find excitement. There is a world of fun, safe, and interesting things out there for him to discover. Can you think of some?**

Most older kids are able to understand this smoking analogy:

Set the scene: **Let's consider what it takes to become addicted to cigarettes.**

Explain the attachment: **Many people who smoke cigarettes started when they were young. People who have researched this say that adult smokers usually began smoking as teenagers because they thought it was cool and wanted to fit in with friends who were also smoking.**

Demonstrate the escalation: **Early smokers say that they liked the way smoking made them feel. Some say it made them feel calmer—especially when they were stressed. However, they said that one cigarette soon lost its effect and they needed to smoke more and more to achieve that same level of calmness.**

Show the addiction: People who smoke so much that they have to take breaks from work, or have a hard time being in a restaurant or movie without smoking, feel terribly anxious if they can't smoke. It can get so bad that they can't go an hour without smoking, and they have to leave stores and other places where they aren't permitted to smoke. Sadly, smoking no longer calms them at all. Instead, it controls them and it's all they can think about. Some people become very sick from smoking, and even when their doctor tells them they might die from it, they don't think they can stop.

Give hope for recovery: The thing is, some of those people choose to get help, and if they work hard, they can stop smoking.

Depending on the age of the child, you may want to give a real life example, that of Evel Knievel:

Set the scene: There was a man named Evel Knievel who enjoyed bike riding.

Explain the attachment: One day

someone showed him how to do a "wheelie." He practiced until he was quite good and soon began doing wheelies while he was riding his bike and standing on the seat—with no hands. He was excited by the danger and liked to show off his skills to his friends.

Demonstrate the escalation: A short time later, Evel saw someone do the same thing—only on a motorcycle. Evel thought if he could do the same thing he might be able to earn some money. So he got a motorcycle and practiced the stunt. He soon found that he got more and more attention by doing increasingly more dangerous stunts.

Elaborate on desensitization: Evel set up a show where people paid to see him putting his life at risk. Even though the stunts were very dangerous, they no longer felt dangerous to Evel because he was constantly looking for the next trick.

Show the addiction: To impress the crowd even more, Mr. Knievel had a twenty-foot-long box filled with rattle-snakes. Then, he tied two lions next to it and told the crowd he would jump across it on his bike. His heart was probably beat-ing fast, but Evel made the jump, and even though his back wheel hit the edge of the box of snakes, he landed and wasn't harmed. He got so much excite-ment from this first jump of his career, that Evel went on to do stunts that often put him in the hospital and almost killed him.

In the longest jump of his career, sail-ing his motorcycle 141 feet over the Caesars Palace fountains in Las Vegas, Evel crashed and sustained major injuries that landed him in the hospital for twenty-nine days. He went on to perform dozens of jumps over the next decade, often with disastrous results. Although he knew that doing the stunts was dangerous and harming him, he couldn't seem to stop.

Give hope for recovery: Evel Knievel eventually un-derstood that his dangerous stunts were damaging his body, so he stopped. How-ever, he died at the young age of 69.

I hope these examples help both you and your child to see the dan-gerous pat-terns of addic-tion. All types of addiction are similar, and they require specific knowledge and insight to overcome. The work is hard, but it can be done.

In the next chapter, we will discuss the steps for you and your child to take to close Pandora's Box, and later in that chapter, we will discuss the best ways to discuss the information you've learned so far with your child.

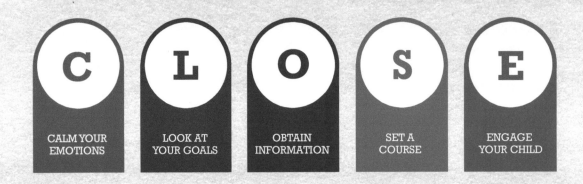

C — CALM YOUR EMOTIONS

L — LOOK AT YOUR GOALS

O — OBTAIN INFORMATION

S — SET A COURSE

E — ENGAGE YOUR CHILD

"It is a matter first of beginning,
and then following through."
– Richard L. Evans

CHAPTER FOUR

Closing Pandora's Box:
A 5-Step Plan for Hope and Healing

The goal of this chapter is to arm you with information, and provide you with direction in working collaboratively *with* your child to become stronger than the lure of pornography, with the ultimate hope of closing Pandora's Box. At the end of this chapter, you will be prepared to sit down with your child and talk about pornography, as well as develop an action plan to successfully fight against it. So let's take a look at the C.L.O.S.E. plan:

Step 1: Calm your emotions

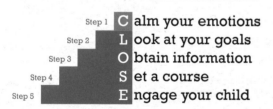

Step 1	**C** alm your emotions
Step 2	**L** ook at your goals
Step 3	**O** btain information
Step 4	**S** et a course
Step 5	**E** ngage your child

One of the most difficult aspects of dealing with your child's exposure to pornography is that the subject can illicit very strong emotions from both of you. As we mentioned in the first chapter, these feelings are completely normal. You can be most effective by learning how to manage these emotions and taking a proactive stance.

Although they are understandable and normal, emotions are the first thing we need to deal with. Our instincts to protect our children are very strong, but our emotional reactions do not always lead us to the best possible actions. In fact, they can often cause further harm to our children. To avoid this, your only option is to step back from the situation and assess your emotions. Think about your child's pornography use. What are you feeling?

Disbelief and denial: "I cannot believe my child would have done this." "Someone else must have downloaded it." "I'll bet it was one of his friends."

Shock: "We have filters. How did this stuff get through them?" "This happens to other people." "How could my child stand to look at this stuff?"

Revulsion: "I can't even think about this, it's so disgusting." "I didn't even know this kind of stuff was out there. It's sickening." "This is more than revolting."

Embarrassment: "I can't talk about this with my child, or anyone." "We'd both be mortified if I mentioned this." "It's too embarrassing." "What would other people think if they knew?"

Shame and guilt: "This is my fault. I should have talked to my teenager about this." "How many other people know about this?" "Parents aren't going to let their kids come over anymore." "I knew I should have been paying closer attention." "Why didn't I put in a filter?"

Blame and anger: "I'm furious!" "I told him to never get into this kind of filth." "What kind of person downloads this stuff?" "He is never going to get on the Internet again. His phone is gone and so is his tablet." "It's his friend's fault. If his parents had been paying attention, this wouldn't have happened."

Fear: "What are we going to do? How bad is it?" "Is she going to turn into some kind of pervert?" "I'm just not equipped to handle this. What am I going to do?" "Once someone gets into looking at this stuff, they can never stop. It's hopeless."

If one or more of these responses sound familiar, you are not alone.

These (and many others!) are the thoughts that parade through our minds when we are confronted with the reality of pornography use by our kids. Your task now is to figure out exactly what you are feeling. Once you know the name of the emotion(s) you're up against, you can begin to dismantle the hold they have on you. Here are some tips for calming these invasive emotions:

• It is important to know that effective communication relies on a balance between our thoughts and emotions. Try to name your emotions and figure out the beliefs that are at their core. Can you use these beliefs or shift them to help you better approach this problem?

• Continually remind yourself how you would want someone to approach you about a sensitive issue. You are not the only one feeling upset about this situation, but you have the power to help guide it in a positive direction.

• Take the compassionate route. How would you feel in your child's position? What is the most helpful role you can play in understanding and dealing with the situation? Facing a problem with pornography is not easy—especially for a child who will likely be both embarrassed and defensive. Think about how you would go about helping one of your friends who became addicted to pornography.

• If less than helpful emotions surface while talking to your child, take a break. Apologize, then start again when everyone's emotions are less negative.

• *Reacting* with negative feelings can push your child away. An emotional reaction limits the available strategies you and your child have for dealing with the situation. In fact, a reactionary approach often makes

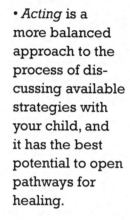

things much worse by adding to the difficult emotions both you and your child are feeling.

• *Acting* is a more balanced approach to the process of discussing available strategies with your child, and it has the best potential to open pathways for healing.

The diagram on the next page stresses the importance of taking time to manage strong emotions before engaging with a child. I find it very useful for parents approaching a highly emotional topic. By following the model of an effective actor, you will be able to keep your emotions under control and maximize the impact of your actions.

Step 2: Look at your goals

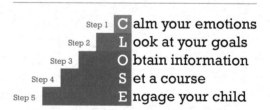

Step 1 **C** alm your emotions
Step 2 **L** ook at your goals
Step 3 **O** btain information
Step 4 **S** et a course
Step 5 **E** ngage your child

Acting is...	Reacting is...

Thoughtful/Slow I'm going to have to think about what I need to do.	***Impulsive/Fast*** We are going to take care of this right now!
Based on Knowledge I need to learn more about this so I'll know what I'm dealing with.	***Based on Emotion*** I am furious! Say goodbye to Internet!
Planned Here are the steps I will take.	***Shoot from the Hip*** I know exactly how I'm going to handle this!
Working Together Let's approach this as a team.	***Dictating*** This is what's going to happen.

Now that you have calmed your emotions, you are in a position to look realistically at what you want to accomplish in talking with your child. Is your goal to help your child learn how harmful porn use can be? Is it to push their behavior underground so as not to get caught? Is it to make them feel bad about themselves? Is it to give your child the knowledge and skill to reject pornography? Is it to change their behavior? Your approach is vital to your goal. Consider the costs and benefits of two different approaches.

As you can see from this exercise, it becomes clear which goals are more effective and beneficial for your child in the long-run. Be honest with yourself about what you want for both you and your child. With that in mind, it will be easier to choose the best goals for your situation.

Anger & Shame Approach		Calm & Informed Approach	
High Costs and Low Benefits		Low Costs and High Benefits	
COSTS	BENEFITS	COSTS	BENEFITS
My child will probably be much more careful so he won't get caught.	I will not have to acknowledge or deal with the situation.	I'll have to get my emotions under control. That's going to take some real work.	My child will probably be much more open to talking about this problem.
I will be removing my ability to have knowledge of, or influence over, their behavior, which may erode my child's trust and confidence in me to help find solutions to problems.	Both of us will be spared the temporary embarrassment of having to talk about pornography use and the damage it can cause.	I'm going to have to do some investigating about my child's porn use.	I'll know more about what I'm dealing with before I talk to my child.
My child will develop deeply shameful feelings, which will make it much more difficult to master this difficult problem.	My child will probably tell me he'll never do it again, which will make me feel better.	I'll need to spend time researching so I can understand porn addiction and how it happens, as well as how to explain it.	I'll have much more information and many more skills to help my child reject pornography.

Next, you will want to make these goals as specific as possible. It will help to write out your goal and determine what information you will need to gather to support this goal. For instance, if your goal is to give your child the knowledge and skill to reject pornography, you'll want to know exactly what knowledge and skills they will need. The following section will go into more detail in explaining the skills, knowledge, and tools available to you and your child.

Step 3: Obtain information

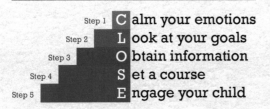

Step 1 **C** alm your emotions
Step 2 **L** ook at your goals
Step 3 **O** btain information
Step 4 **S** et a course
Step 5 **E** ngage your child

It is very important to obtain information you can use to help you and your child get through the sensitive issue of pornography use. Here is the information I use with the parents and children I treat. I consider the following five tools to be essential:

Part A: The W Questions

Before you begin to help your child, it is important to have as much information as possible about the situation. By directly asking your child the "W" questions, or investigating them ahead of time, you will be able to further define the best actions to take to help your child.

Who?

Is there someone who exposed your child to pornography? If this person can be identified (in my experience, it is often a friend, babysitter, family member or extended family member), it is important to intervene in their contact with your child. Depending on the age and the relationship of the person who exposed your child to porn, you may have to alert someone who has influence over that person, such as law enforcement, a parent, or school official.

Answering the *Who* question is important because continued and/or unsupervised contact with someone who has introduced your child to pornography only increases continued access and exposure. In certain cases, knowing who is behind a child viewing pornography is vital to keeping them safe from predators.

What?

On what device is the child accessing pornography? It is essential that this be determined. Most kids access porn on handheld devices like tablets or phones. However, others view it via laptops, video games, PCs, television, and movies. It's absolutely necessary for parents to, as much as possible, restrict any access to pornography. Continued access only strengthens the hold porn has over its victim.

When?

Knowing when a child is viewing porn is, once again, essential to precluding access. Is it at night when everyone is sleeping? Is it during the summertime when children may be alone all day (studies show a dramatic increase in searches for porn during this time)? Is it after school? Is it during a sleepover when the kids are unsupervised?

Where?

At what location is the child accessing porn? Is it at home, a friend's house, at school, the library? Discovering where the child is being exposed to pornography is essential to stopping their access to it.

Why?

There are many answers to the question of why your child is viewing porn, but children aren't likely to know them—so parents should refrain from asking this one. However, here are a few possibilities you should discuss with your child:

• Children are curious and they don't have the skills to reject porn when they see it. A child's curiosity is often much stronger than we think. Sex is a natural lure—even during childhood. The older we get, the more sexual feelings we appropriately develop, but children and adolescents are not prepared for the sexual feelings they come to associate with pornography.

• They may not understand how to say no to a friend or someone else who is exposing them to it.

• They may not know how to control their own desire to view porn. As you will see in the *Two States of Mind Model* to follow, the emotional state of mind can easily begin to take the lead when a child is short on logic, reason, and rational decision-making skills.

• They may think that they just can't stop using pornography. Repeated exposure to pornography and its triggers increases the control it has over your child.

• Most adults report feeling drawn to porn when they feel bored, stressed, lonely or upset. We are finding this to be true for children, as well.

The list can stretch pretty long, but helping a child understand some of the most common reasons they turn to porn can help them deal with these triggers on an individual level.

The exercise on the following page can help a child identify feelings they have before they turn to pornography and what they can do instead. This example is filled in with some trigger ideas. A blank copy of the exercise can be found at the back of the book.

Emotional Triggers

Here are some of the feelings I have before I look at pornography:

- I am bored

- I am mad at my friend

- I am tired of being told to sweep the floor

- When my parents see my grades I am going to be in a lot of trouble

- Porn makes me feel better

Alternative Solutions

Here are some things I can do about those feelings:

- Play basketball

- Talk to someone about the problem

- Sweep the floor (If I do not, I will get in trouble and still have to sweep it)

- Face up to the grades (If I use porn, the grades will still be a problem)

- Immediately get away from the device that is tempting me (In the end, porn will not make me feel any better)

Next, we have to understand a little bit about the brain because it's very important in understanding how an addiction to pornography starts. The method I like to use involves brain structures that impact youthful emotion and logic.

We can essentially boil down how we process information by looking at how we think (illogically or logically) and how we process how we feel (emotionally). These comprise the *Two States of Mind.*

• A *Logical State of Mind* involves information, fact, evidence, reason, and objectivity. It assists us in thinking through situations and responding to them in a planned manner. The logical state of mind has the potential to keep us safe, because it takes information and processes it in a manner that results in judgment.

• An *Emotional State of Mind* is relatively simple to describe. It's all about how we *feel* and the choices we make based upon those feelings. We are hardwired to want things that make us feel good. Food, nurturance, closeness, and intimacy are some of the most basic desires because they ensure our survival—now and in the future.

A balanced combination of the two states of mind can keep us safe while getting what we want and need. The problem is, children and teens sometimes rely almost exclusively on their emotional state of mind because the logical state of mind is underdeveloped, and may not be fully formed until late adolescence or even young adulthood. That's why teens jump off two-story buildings into swimming pools, drive recklessly, and engage in other risky behaviors without a care in the world. The logical mind has not come into play and it's all about emotion and the "high" the immature person gets from reckless or unsafe behavior.

An experience from my own life illustrates my point perfectly. As adolescents, my cousin and I decided that it was a good idea to get into a shopping cart we'd found and ride it down a hill (pure emotional state of mind). Any logical state of mind must have been left at home, because off we went, careening down a hill that was much steeper than we'd thought, and was becoming increasingly dangerous the faster we went.

What we didn't know about the physics of speed, a narrow wheel base, and wobbly wheels cost me quite a bit of skin, and my cousin several front teeth. In the end, we learned Newton's first law of motion: "An object in motion stays in motion with the same speed in the same direction unless acted upon by an unbalanced force," which for us was gravity and rocky asphalt. Newton's law appeals to a logical state of mind. Getting into a grocery cart on a steep hill does not.

So, let's look at how an emotional state of mind, without the moderating influence of a logical state of mind, applies to a child's use of pornography.

The Two States of Mind and Pornography

When a child is exposed to pornography, they experience a strong rush of sexual emotion that makes them feel good. Children are unaware of the addictive properties of the drug called pornography. They don't understand that just because something feels exciting, it may not be good for them. They simply don't understand that they are going downhill and into something that has the potential to harm them and take over their life.

That's where parents come in. They understand the dangers of pornography and its addictive power. They understand cause and effect. They possess information they can teach

to their children. The adage of "information is power" could not apply more appropriately to this situation. You can teach the power of judgment. You can teach your child to draw on the logical state of mind to balance out the pull of the emotional one.

Remember, you taught your child the dangers of touching a hot surface. You can do the same thing when you find that your child is accessing porn. With guidance from parents in the process of maturation and learning, children can develop the ability to balance the logical and emotional states of their minds, which can be a very powerful tool in mastering the pull of pornography.

The Two States of Mind and Addiction

When addiction is involved, the logical state of mind can be overrun by the emotional state of mind, which no longer accepts input from a mind that is unaware (or doesn't seem to care) that something isn't good for us. When it comes to pornography, this means that the logical mind is no longer able to warn the emotional mind of the dangers associated with continuing to seek out this very potent drug.

Knowing this, one of your goals should focus on helping your child understand that emotions alone can lead them astray, whereas logic and judgment have the potential to keep feelings that could lead to problems

in check. When your child understands this, you and your child can develop strategies to manage their feelings and behavior by giving their logical state of mind the power it needs to reject the pull of pornography. I use a particular exercise to help the people I treat understand that when it comes to pornography, skills related to logic and judgment can be powerful in managing its extremely strong pull.

The Two States of Mind Bubble Diagram

The goal of this exercise is for you and your child to understand the emotion tied to pornography use, as well as how judgment and skill can balance its unrelenting pull. The exercise typically turns out best when parents and children complete it together, but older children may want to work on it alone and talk about it later.

As you can see, the diagram on the next page has two overlapping circles. One represents the logical mind and the other represents the emotional mind. Since pornography appeals almost exclusively to emotion, the left circle contains, "Pornography makes me feel good." Emotion, which is very strong in the case of this addictive material, fills up the entire circle. However, the Logical Mind circle contains what we can use to manage the powerful emotions tied to pornography use. The overlapping part of the circles shows how logic and judgment have the potential to balance out the emotion: "Just because something feels good, doesn't mean it's good for me."

The diagram below is an example of how this form might look once it's completed. You may want to use this exercise after you and your child have become familiar with some of the other skills you will learn as you keep reading. You will find a blank copy of this form at the back of the book.

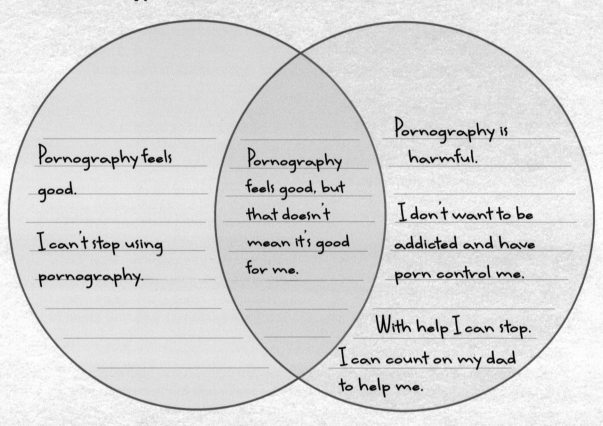

The important takeaway from this particular exercise is the recognition that there are two separate and valid states of mind. We must teach them to work together for our benefit.

Another interactive strategy that ties into the Two States of Mind Model is the Act vs. React exercise. Only this time, you and your child will work together learning how they can ACT instead of REACT when confronted with pornography or the temptation to use it. We will discuss the STOP plan you'll see later. A blank copy of this exercise can be found at the back of the book.

Acting is...	Reacting is...
Thoughtful/Slow I'm going to have to think about what I need to do.	**_Impulsive/Fast_** Turn on my phone and download it now.
Based on Knowledge I can get addicted to this stuff.	**_Based on Emotion_** Porn makes me feel good.
Planned I'll use my STOP plan.	**_No Planning_** I'll figure it out on my own.

Part C: Thinking Errors vs. Protective Barriers Model

This is another tool that can help children understand how we can make errors in judgment. When we want something, we all have a tendency to override our logical mind by justifying whatever it is that the emotional mind wants. Knowing this can help you understand what may be influencing your child's pornography use, and help your child recognize and reject the "thinking errors" that work against behavior change.

One of our jobs is to protect our children. We place locks on cabinets that have cleaning supplies in them when our children are infants. We have a fence around the backyard where children are playing. We put locks on our doors to prevent the wrong people from coming into our homes.

These are physical barriers to keep our children safe.

Other barriers are internal and usually involve teaching and modeling values. For instance, we teach a toddler that hitting is wrong because it hurts others. We teach our children not to steal and to respect laws. To help our children lead healthy and productive lives, we spend time helping them understand what is right and what is wrong, what can keep them safe, the consequences of inappropriate behavior, and an awareness of things that can harm them.

I don't steal because I was taught it is wrong. That is a protective barrier. *I could get caught.* That is a protective barrier. *I could lose my freedom.* That is a protective barrier. *I would be embarrassed for my friends and family to find out that I was a thief.*

That's a protective barrier. Sometimes though, children, adolescents, and adults get around those barriers by using the thinking errors of rationalizing, justifying, minimizing, and blaming. Thinking errors are simply ways of avoiding responsibility for our behavior.

Take speeding for example. When I speed, I know I'm breaking the law, which I've been taught is wrong because people could get hurt. But by engaging my thinking errors I get around feeling bad. *I'm late to work and I have to be there on time.* That is a thinking error. *I'm a good driver. No one will get hurt.* That is a thinking error. *Everyone speeds. It's just part of driving.* That's a thinking error. *If my daughter would have filled up the car like she said she would, I wouldn't have had to stop and get gas.* Yep, thinking error.

To help your child understand thinking errors in the context of pornography use, you might want to use the following diagram to provide examples of these two types of thinking. You will find a blank version at the back of the book for your personal use.

Encourage your child to come up with some examples from their own life and encourage them to think about how these types of thinking helped or hurt their situation.

Thinking Errors

Rationalizing/Justifying

"Everyone looks at porn."

"It's just part of growing up."

Minimizing

"It's not hurting anyone."

"It's no big deal."

"It's just pictures."

"I can stop anytime I want to."

Blaming

"If my parents didn't want me to look at porn, they should have put in filters."

"If my friend hadn't shown porn to me, I wouldn't be using it."

"It's society's fault for allowing this stuff to be out there."

Barriers that Protect

Porn can be addictive—just like a drug.

I'd be embarrassed and ashamed if I got caught.

My parents would be really disappointed in me.

It can harm my relationships.

It's not just pictures. These are real people. They may look happy, but many of them say they feel used and bad about themselves.

My behavior is under my control.

Part D: The Cost/Benefit Method

Later in this chapter, you will learn how to share all of this information with your child. For now, I'd like to arm you with a couple of methods you can pass on to your child to help them cope in the face of pornography use. Once you explain the *Two States of Mind Model* and the *Thinking Errors vs. Protective Barriers Model* with your child, they will begin to understand how their mind works in relation to porn, and hopefully acknowledge that they are in control of their own mind and what they do.

At this point, you can let them know that there are specific ways they can control their mind and behavior. The first way to do that is to give them an opportunity on their own to evaluate the costs and benefits of stopping pornography use. Having learned about the risks of addiction and the dangers of pornography to their growth and development, your child should be able to fill out the full-page *Costs and Benefits of Stopping Pornography Use* worksheet at the back of this book. Below, you can see an example of how this might look.

Costs and Benefits of Stopping Pornography Use

Costs	Benefits
I will no longer have the good feelings that pornography gives me.	I won't be addicted and rely on pornography to make me feel good. I will be able to pay attention to many other things that interest me.
I will be curious and it will be difficult to stop my curiosity.	I will feel stronger knowing that I can control my own mind and body.
This will be something I will have to work hard at.	I will have healthy attitudes about sex and will develop coping skills to help me throughout my life.

This is a tool I typically use for younger people struggling with pornography use, though some adolescents like the visual aspect. It involves the child making a stop sign and then visualizing it in their mind when they are exposed to, tempted by, or are in the process of viewing pornography. Most kids enjoy coloring and decorating it. For adolescents, I ask them to see a stop sign in their mind that includes the words on the diagram.

Stop looking at the device
Think about how pornography harms
Open the logical part of my mind
Proceed with my plan

We'll talk more about the "Plan" in Step 4 (Set a course). You can find this important tool in the form of both a coloring page and a visual representation at the back of the book.

Above all else, know that you and your child are not alone. According to some of the latest research on "The Nature and Dynamics of Internet Pornography Exposure for Youth," by the age of 18, 90% of boys and 60% of

girls have been exposed to Internet porn. Most of the people I treat for pornography addiction say they were exposed before the age of twelve— with some reporting exposure as young as six.

Don't forget that many other parents are experiencing this same problem. Your child is not an awful or immoral person and you are not an awful parent. It's about a multi-billion-dollar industry going after children by exposing them to a highly addictive form of media. By going after children, the porn industry hopes to develop life-long addicts, with no concern about the long-term effects of immature minds ingesting their emotionally and physically damaging material. Just remember, as a parent you can teach your child how to draw on the logical part of their mind, which will help both of you develop and use skills to fight the enticing power of pornography.

Step 4: Set a course

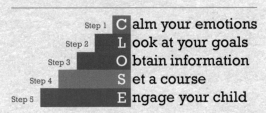

Step 1	**C**alm your emotions
Step 2	**L**ook at your goals
Step 3	**O**btain information
Step 4	**S**et a course
Step 5	**E**ngage your child

You have your goals in place, and you have a toolbox of information and strategies to help you help your child reject pornography. Now it's time to prepare yourself to share this information with your child. It is important to remember that talking about this issue should not occur in one sitting. Pay attention to your child so that you can recognize signs (anger, frustration, etc.) that might indicate when to take a break and start again at another time. The younger the child, the more important it is to address the issue of pornography in bite-sized pieces.

With your goals in mind, it's time to prepare a script that will set the stage for positive communication, help you keep your emotions in check, and provide information in a supportive, compassionate, and positive manner. In this step, you will learn how to consolidate the information presented earlier in this chapter, and actually write out a script identifying your personal goals for your child and the information you would like to convey.

Before you talk with your child, make sure you are approaching the conversation with the right information and frame of mind. The following checklist can help you do this:

☐ I have calmed my emotions. I understand that neither myself nor my child are to blame.

☐ I have looked at my goals and identified the goals that will best help my child.

☐ I understand that I want to ACT, not REACT.

☐ I have obtained as much information as possible by researching the W Questions.

☐ I have read and understand the *Two States of Mind Model*.

☐ I have read and understand the *Thinking Errors vs. Protective Barriers Model*.

☐ I am prepared to discuss the *Cost/Benefit Method* with my child.

☐ I am prepared to discuss the *STOP Pornography Method* with my child.

If you've checked off everything on the list, congratulations! You are ready to move on.

The next step is to create a script for your conversation. Don't let this scare you. It doesn't have to be a formal script and it can take any form you are comfortable with. The point here is that you identify and remember all of the main topics you wish to discuss with your child. It is also important to recognize that your initial conversation is just the beginning, that you will likely not get through all the information in one sitting. You will have many conversations as you and your child work through this problem. If you plan carefully, this initial script should help guide you through the process of working with your child to reject pornography.

You can use the following worksheet, also found at the back of the book, to generate the essential talking points you wish to review with your child.

Pornography Discussion Script

Opener *How will you open the conversation? Remember to remain calm and stress the importance of working together. Don't forget to include your goals.*

_____

_____

Explaining Addiction *What example(s) will you use to explain the cycle of addiction to your child?*

_____

_____

Parental Checkpoint

☐ I am remaining calm and objective

☐ I have reminded my child that looking at pornography does not make them "bad"

Encouraging Your Child's Perspective *How will you invite your child to participate in the conversation? Consider some questions that will encourage them to share their thoughts and feelings about pornography and addiction.*

_____

_____

Explaining the Mind *What example(s) will you use to illustrate the Two States of Mind Model?*

_____

_____

Uniting Concepts *How will you introduce the Two States of Mind Bubble Diagram (appendix A) and encourage your child to consider how the two states of mind act in relation to pornography?*

_____

_____

Working Together *What will you say and do to show your child that you want to work together on this problem? What will you say and do to encourage your child's input into a plan to reject pornography?*

_____

_____

Step 5: Engage your child

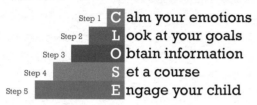

Step 1 **C** alm your emotions
Step 2 **L** ook at your goals
Step 3 **O** btain information
Step 4 **S** et a course
Step 5 **E** ngage your child

Now that you have completed the preliminary work, take a deep breath. You are ready to broach an open and productive conversation with your child!

The final step to closing Pandora's Box is to actively engage your child in discussing pornography and creating an action plan to reject it.

With your script prepared and worksheets in hand, sit down with your child in a non-threatening and non-judgmental way and let him or her know you would like to talk about a common problem: pornography. Reassure them that you love and want to help them, so as to reduce their embarrassment and shame as much as possible. With the right information and approach, you can both be successful.

Remember that this is not a time to be hard on your child or yourself. No conversation ever goes exactly according to plan. Your child has not had the time and space you have had to consider this issue objectively, and may respond emotionally. Here are some likely reactions you can be prepared for:

Embarrassment The subject of pornography is typically embarrassing for a child or teen (and parents, as well), and the older they get, the more resistance you might meet. Unfortunately, the first time most parents talk to their child about pornography is after the child has already been exposed to it, so your child is already feeling the tumult of emotions that you yourself went through earlier.

Lying and Denying Be prepared for your child to deny downloading and viewing porn (it's not theirs; someone else downloaded it; they would never do that; a friend must have done it—this is normal). Understand that even if they admit to viewing porn, they will likely minimize it; some may even continue to deny viewing it, so talk about the importance of honesty, but only in the context of helping. There is nothing to be gained by debating this issue. Your child will simply become more entrenched in the lie, because to be honest is to make him look like an even bigger liar. Expecting this reaction can keep you from experiencing additional anger or frustration while talking with your child.

If either you or your child become angry or reach an impasse, take a time-out and come back to it when emotions have calmed. Above all else, remember that it is often not what we talk about, but *how* we talk about it, that makes the biggest difference.

The results of this and other conversations about pornography can be life-changing, so try to keep in mind the following key ingredients for success:

• Express love and concern and a willingness to work together to learn how to combat pornography's dangerous pull.

• Educate your child about the risks of pornography and addiction in an age-appropriate manner.

• There is no perfect solution for everybody. Develop an individual plan that focuses on particular skills your child can draw on to resist the lure of pornography.

• Work collaboratively in setting goals and developing strategies that fit your child and their stage of development.

• Discuss the steps you plan to take and the potential of your child coming into contact with this harmful material. As much as possible, it is essential that parents attempt to prevent further access to pornography.

Before we get into creating an action plan, we need to focus on and reiterate the importance of preventing your child's access to pornography.

Preventing Access to Pornography
At this point you might be wondering about steps you can take to stop your child's access to pornography. There are a number of ways to do this. You can disconnect the Internet during unsupervised times when your child might attempt to access porn. Some parents put passwords on all electronic devices and remove Internet capability on cell phones. Cell phones were originally developed for making phone calls, yet they have become the primary tool for adolescents (and adults) to access pornography. Consider this: Your child doesn't require the Internet to make phone calls. Many parents simply purchase phones that are just that, phones. Another strategy is to call your cell provider for help in blocking access to the Internet. For too many kids, having devices that allow

unsupervised and unfettered access to the Internet is a dangerous thing. There are many filtering programs to screen out pornography on Internet-capable devices. Parents need to know, however, that the porn industry hires very skilled people whose job is to get around filter programs. Unfortunately, they are having great success. The companies that develop filter programs have to constantly update their programs because of how quickly the porn industry gets around them. It is vital that you update a filter program when an update is available.

Remember, a screening program is only one safeguard, but don't make the mistake of believing it covers all other means of access. Some companies have developed "accountability software" that include a report of what sites have been visited, by whom, at what time and for how long. Many programs limit actual access to the Internet and put parental restrictions on devices for downloading apps, movies and other material. But don't forget, the porn industry is working *right now* to get around all types of programs that attempt to limit access to their harmful material. One last thing about filter programs: they use words to screen out pornography, but they can't screen out *images or live streaming of pornographic acts*. The technology simply doesn't exist.

It is very important to know that some children, and particularly adolescents, have become very adept at getting around programs that attempt to block pornography. Keep in mind that you may be able to block Internet use at home, but if a cell phone or device has Internet capability, all a child or adolescent has to do is go to places where there is unrestricted access to the Internet (restaurants, stores, friends' and relatives' homes, churches, school and other places).

It is very common that kids are exposed to or have access to pornography at friends' houses—particularly after school and sleepovers—where they are unsupervised. Some parents may feel it is drastic, but I advise against sleepovers. I have seen too many children who report that their initial exposure to pornography occurred during overnight stays with friends and even relatives. Even more distressing is that a number of the boys and girls I treat for sexual abuse report that the abuse occurred at a sleepover.

Some parents put cell phones and tablets in a basket when friends come over and give them back when they leave. Keep in mind, though, that blocking the Internet won't have any effect if a friend or other person visiting your home has already downloaded pornography on their device.

So many parents ask me if they should totally take away a phone or tablet, and if they do, for how long. That is one of the most difficult questions for me to answer because it depends on so many factors. To help determine if your child is ready to responsibly have access to the Internet, you might want to consider these questions:

Has your child acknowledged a problem with pornography? Is he or she working on the problem? Is your child cooperating with the restrictions you placed on the Internet? Can they give you some examples of what to do when they're tempted to view pornography? Ultimately, our children have to have the opportunity to use the skills we've taught them. That can't happen if they have no Internet access. I advise parents to keep appropriate restrictions (filters, parental controls, etc.) even while allowing their children to show they can responsibly function in a digital world. Some final advice on access: When your child returns to Internet use, they may have slips or relapses. Expect that this may happen because relapses are common. That's why it is

so important to talk about rejecting pornography often. Finishing this book and the exercises in it is not enough. Regularly checking in with your child, talking about how they're doing and reinforcing their action plan can go a long way toward preventing a relapse or working through one if it happens. It is vital to talk early about this problem and talk often. And don't forget, working together in learning how to reject pornography is a process, not an event.

Creating an Action Plan

Once you and your child have discussed all the information on the Pornography Discussion Script, you can begin to generate your action plan. By now, your child should understand how dangerous pornography is and should be equipped with some methods for resisting its lure. The next thing is to help your child outline some specific actions he or she can take to win pornography's ongoing tug of war.

Armed with this essential information, it is now time to visualize your success. Putting your commitment in writing can be tremendously powerful. The following action plan form is for the child and parent to fill out together, keeping in mind that there is no shame in being accountable for a problem, and only strength to be gained from identifying and overcoming it. You will find copies of this form at the back of the book for your personal use.

My Action Plan (Child)

I am accessing porn on these devices

_____

_____

_____

I am accessing porn at these places & times

_____

_____

_____

To limit physical access to pornography I will

_____

_____

_____

Before I view porn I often feel

_____

_____

_____

Here are some things I can do about those feelings

_____

_____

_____

When I view porn I feel

_____

_____

_____

After I view porn I feel

_____

_____

_____

Some alternatives to pornography that also make me feel good are

_____

_____

_____

_____

I can use my logical state of mind to help me stop looking at porn by

_____

_____

_____

When I am tempted to look at porn I will take the following actions

_____

_____

_____

I can reduce my thinking errors by reminding myself of the barriers that help protect me, such as

_____

_____

_____

I can see a stop sign in my head and know that it's there to protect me. When I see this stop sign and act accordingly I feel

_____

_____

_____

The costs of using porn are

_____

_____

_____

I want to stop viewing porn because

_____

_____

_____

My parents can help support me by

_____

_____

_____

_____

As we've learned so far, it is vital that you and your child take action in eliminating porn use. As we discussed earlier, this is a societal issue and no one is alone in this battle. Just as it is important not to place blame on either yourself or your child, it is important that you both demonstrate accountability for the actions you take. Together, your family can form a unified front against pornography use. There is, undeniably, strength in unity.

The problem of pornography has a better chance of being defeated when we take a stand and make a commitment. The worksheet on the next page will help you remember what you need to know and what you plan to do in working with your child to defeat pornography's hold on your child.

If you prepare, ask for your child's input, accept their contributions, make a plan, and follow that plan, you have the potential to make a lasting impact on your child's future and their ability to deal with a problem that could otherwise spiral out of control.

My Action Plan (Parent)

My child has access to porn on these devices
_____

My child has access to porn at these places and times
_____

To limit physical access to pornography I will
_____

When I recognize that my child is struggling with resisting pornography
and/or struggling with appropriate coping techniques, I will
_____

I will set a positive example by
_____

I will encourage safe Internet usage in our home by
_____

I will encourage my child to feel safe and to continue to discuss pornography use
with me by
_____

The costs of using porn are
_____

I want my child to stop viewing porn because
_____

I will support my child by
_____
_____
_____
_____
_____
_____

"There is a great deal of sexual
stimulation in modern culture, and
children have greater knowledge
of (but not necessarily a greater
understanding) and exposure
to sexual behavior today than in
previous generations."
– Toni Cavanagh Johnson, Ph.D.

CHAPTER FIVE

Putting the Lid on Porn:
Understanding Your Role in Fighting Pornography Use

It's all well and good to talk about changes, but the real change comes when we follow through on our commitments. The 5-step CLOSE Plan you learned about in Chapter Four is designed to help us make those commitments to ourselves and our children.

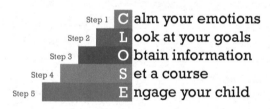

Step 1	**C** alm your emotions
Step 2	**L** ook at your goals
Step 3	**O** btain information
Step 4	**S** et a course
Step 5	**E** ngage your child

The key is to take action on the information you learn and the plans you come up with, and repeat the steps over and over until your child is free from the damaging effects of pornography. The difficulty in dealing with childhood use of pornography is that we never know how our children will react to exposure or what will work best for them in resisting it until we actively wage this battle. However, we do know that certain types of parenting have correlations with the emotional and behavioral health of children. So what are they?

Parenting Styles

Three social scientists set out to learn just this. They wanted to explore how parents influence adolescent problem behaviors, so they asked 2,568 high school students (ages 14-18) to complete questionnaires about their involvement in delinquent behaviors and substance abuse, as well as their perceptions of parental warmth, control, monitoring of activities, and knowledge of where their adolescent was, what they were doing, and who they were with. The findings suggest that "parental warmth and monitoring deter adolescent involvement in problem behavior."

What better evidence for the encouraging fact that we do have an impact on how our children choose to live their lives? So, you may be asking, what do these quality parental influences look like? Let's take a look:

The Monitoring Parent

Parents who ask questions and set guidelines and limitations over their children's behavior tend to be more informed about the lives of their kids. Well-informed parents tend to have children who are less likely to engage in problem behaviors.

The Warm Parent

Parental warmth encourages children to be more open with their parents and have a more positive relationship with them. This, in turn, leads to greater parental knowledge about their children's lives, and deters problem behaviors.

For years, social scientists have been studying how parents interact with their children. Based on the results of hundreds of studies, researchers and practitioners have come to accept that there are basically three styles of parenting: permissive, authoritative and authoritarian.

Using decades of research, we now know which style typically produces the best results when it comes to child adjustment. As you think about each style, consider which one has the most likelihood of success when it comes to helping your child reject pornography.

The Permissive Parent

Permissive parents allow their children a great deal of freedom and rarely restrict their behavior. They tend to be indulgent. Children of these parents are typically left to manage their own behavior and receive little discipline. Without discipline, they fail to learn personal responsibility, usually have more problem behaviors and are more susceptible to negative peer pressure.

The Authoritative Parent

Authoritative parents set limits and have rules to guide their child's behavior. They teach accountability and the consequences of certain behaviors. Parents who rear children in an authoritative manner spend more time communicating with them and teaching decision-making skills. As a result, these children often have higher self-esteem, better academic success, and fewer behavioral problems.

Authoritarian Parenting

Authoritarian parents demand obedience from their children without encouraging reciprocal communication. They tend to focus on punishment in an attempt to break the child's behavior, without explaining to the child why their behavior is unacceptable. The children of authoritarian parents tend to have low self-esteem, higher levels of stress, and difficulty trusting due to the shaming they receive under this parenting style.

From these descriptions, we can clearly see that the authoritative parenting style values the child's healthy growth and development above all else and achieves the best results in doing so. Research cited in the Journal of Education and Human Development has shown that this style has the best potential to promote individuality, self-regulation, and assertiveness by being supportive of a child's needs and demands.

We all have our own unique style of parenting, but by understanding your child's needs, evaluating their behaviors objectively, and communicating effective solutions, you can maximize your opportunities to teach them and have them internalize lessons that will see them through life.

Communicating with Your Child

Whatever your parenting style, it is important to take care when handling the most formative issues of your child's life. Approaching these events with effective communication skills in hand can ensure they will get the most benefit from these interactions.

To encourage open communication between yourself and your child, focus on listening to them with a spirit of acceptance and non-judgment. Ask them questions and pay attention to the answers. Show them that you understand their feelings and listen by repeating what you hear and asking follow-up questions. Children may not readily talk about their feelings, but try to be aware of them and set a compassionate stage so they will feel safe if they do want to talk about them.

Once again, it is important to stop when emotions start to overrun the conversation or things become heated. You can return to the conversation later when things are calmer. You and your child may not always see eye to eye, but helping your child to set healthy boundaries for themselves and fostering an atmosphere of acceptance will ultimately influence their behavior more positively than other forms of discipline or permissiveness.

The Sexualized Home

How sexualized is your home? This may not be something you immediately consider, because our adult understanding of what constitutes a sexualized environment may be much different than a child's.

According to Toni Cavanagh Johnson, Ph.D., in *Helping Children with Sexual Behavior Problems: A Guidebook for Professionals and Caregivers*, there are three primary areas that can contribute to a sexualized home:

Sexualized Content
Children are especially susceptible and attracted to television shows, books, magazines, songs and videos with even mild doses of sexual content. Consider the things your child is listening to, watching or reading and try to look at the content from their point of view. A bombardment of sexual material can create a desire in the emotional mind to seek out further stimulation. That doesn't mean we don't talk about sex. What's important is that your child isn't overly exposed to sexual media when they don't have the logical capacity to understand what's good and what is bad for them.

Sexualized Interactions
Consider the types of interactions your child is exposed to in regard to hygiene, affection, and privacy in the home. Does your child see adults or older children naked in your home? In what ways is privacy respected and maintained? Whenever possible, teach your child the importance of respecting their bodies as their own private property, and show them the importance of both setting and respecting boundaries.

Sexualized Speech
Pay close attention to the way you or others speak around your children. Our kids pick up on so much more than we think. Jokes, comments and words with sexual connotations may resonate with them on a level we have become desensitized to. If you hear your child making inappropriate comments or jokes of a sexual nature, take it as an opportunity to teach them how to set boundaries, not only in their actions, but also their words.

Take a moment to consider how your child might be interpreting things they read, see and hear. Don't forget that children imitate what they see. We may not be able to change the sexually inappropriate material our children are surrounded with outside our homes, but we can make our homes places where our children are not flooded with overly sexualized material. If we don't want our child's sexual development shaped by the world's pervasive deluge of all things sexual, we can at least take a look at what type of material we invite into our homes. It's our job to help our children develop healthy sexual attitudes, but if what is in our homes contradicts them, it's going to be a tough sell.

Fighting Pornography at Home and Beyond

I can't say this enough: Kids know more about electronics than we think they do! If you were shocked to discover that your child has accessed pornography, you may also be alarmed at how easy it is for them to do so, despite what you think you have

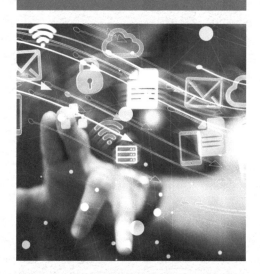

done to stop it. Many of us think that our home computers and devices are fairly well-protected, whether we've gone the extra step to put restricting software on them or simply believe that we are effectively monitoring usage. Considering that somewhere near 81% of teens who've accessed pornography have done so at home, this can be a rude awakening as to the steps we've taken (or not taken) to protect them.

When installing software, it's important to do so across all devices. Re-

portedly, only "28% of parents have installed software on computers to prohibit certain website visitation, only 17% have the same software on mobile devices." Additionally, you will want to learn how the software works so that you can maximize its effectiveness. Many parents let parental controls go unused simply because they don't know how to access or operate them. I must insert a very important point here: Do not trust parental controls or a filtering program to manage access to pornography. Consider the following scenario:

A 5th grade teacher called Technical Support in her school and said, "My computer isn't working. It's broken."

The technician asked, "How do you know it's broken?"

The teacher replied, "One of my students told me."

Said the technician? "I'll be right there."

Young children are often "smarter" than adults when it comes to electronics. They, or one of their friends, can often find ways around filters. Kids—especially older ones—know all about apps that can lead to inappropriate information. They also know about apps that can instantly delete offensive material from their phones and other devices. This makes it even more difficult for parents to track what their children are doing online.

Once again, remember these important points:

• Unless parental controls are activated on portable, Internet-enabled *devices*, kids can get access to the Internet in fast-food restaurants, libraries, friends' houses or at other places where there is public access. Parents must have information about how to limit Internet access on portable devices. With respect to cell phones, make sure the parental controls you use explicitly state that they work on cellular connections.

• A filter program at home is *only* effective at home.

• The porn industry hires the best in computer minds to find ways to beat filter programs, and they're good at it. They have billions of dollars to spend on getting around your filtering program.

• Filter programs use *words* to prevent porn from invading Internet-capable devices. They cannot recognize or filter out pornographic *images*—the human body or what it's doing.

• Parents must keep up with potentially dangerous apps available to children. There are controls parents can use where downloading apps require their permission. However, parents must research apps before approving their download. A child may want an app that appears innocuous, when it is really something you don't want your child having access to.

• Parents must understand the limitations of filter/blocking programs and not rely on them as a sole strategy to protect their children from pornography.

• Parents must continuously update filtering programs because of how fast the porn industry gets around them.

• If you don't understand any of the above, take the time to talk to an expert. Call filtering companies and ask to speak to someone who can explain their products. Choose a program you believe best meets your needs, and one you can fully understand, install and manage.

• Contact your mobile device company to learn how to manage the Internet on a cell phone.

• Keep informed. Precluding access to pornography is a process, not an event. Keeping up with technology is paramount.

Remember that it is not enough to simply restrict your child from using the Internet. In today's digital age, children should be taught to interact appropriately with this media in order to foster competence and self-worth.

You taught your child how to act around those cleaning supplies we talked about earlier, knowing that one day the cabinet would be unlocked and they would have access to them. In the same way, we should be actively teaching our children about Internet safety, as well as coping mechanisms, to ensure that they know how to engage with the Internet and avoid some of its most harmful materials. Physical barriers are a temporary solution. Knowledge, coping skills and the development of *internal* barriers have the potential to become permanent.

Beyond the Home

As we discussed in Chapter Three, pornography addiction can cause behavioral changes in children, prompting sexual behaviors. An increase in desensitized children and sexual deviance among our youth poses a serious public health risk.

While creating change within the home is a great first step, there are measures we can take on a larger scale to limit access to pornography and reduce sexual behavior problems among our youth. Raising awareness and supporting legislation that attempts to limit pornography exposure, while still protecting First Amendment rights, can make a large-scale difference in how we view and solve this problem.

"With the Internet, the protective barrier between the sex industry and youth dissolved and the home, historically considered a safe haven, has been the very place where the sex industry is grooming our youth."
– Dr. Jill Manning

CHAPTER SIX

Recovery and Maintenance: *Revisiting Your Skills Often*

When facing your own child's pornography use, the problem can seem daunting. But we would all do well to remember Pandora and her box, and the fact that hope was found in it. She was not to blame for her inquisitive nature, and neither are you or your child to blame for what can be found on any Internet-enabled device. While there are forces beyond our control when it comes to the prevalence of pornography, you can still be a force for positive change.

It's important to note that there is no foolproof plan for eliminating pornography. There are times when even a parent's best efforts are not enough to keep their child from seeking out or being exposed to pornography. Whether viewing pornography for the first time or revisiting it after a span of time, seeing your child struggle with its lure – after all of the hard work you've done together – can be very discouraging. However, please do not give up. If your child relaps-

es, it's more important than ever to keep your cool and keep the lines of communication open. After all, we've already learned that it's natural for children to be attracted to the dangerous world of pornography. If we can convey that, it will be easier to reduce shame. If we reduce shame, it is more likely that our child will talk to us about this difficult topic.

Although it may be uncomfortable, it is vital that parents revisit the topic of pornography use often, even after it appears to be under control. Continue to think about and update your action plans, and consider new ways to meet the threat head-on. As your child grows, their access to pornography will likely change, as will the ever-lengthening reach of the porn industry. Stay informed, stay alert, and help your child continue to stay safe. Here are a few check-in items that are important to cover on a regular basis:

• Find out if and when your child has been tempted to relapse and view porn.

• Test your Internet filters and check to see if there are new filters that might better meet your needs.

• Revisit the tools you and your child have learned to help them in rejecting porn. Ask for examples of when and how these have been useful.

• Ask your child about the activities they find most rewarding. As your child grows, it is increasingly important to help direct them toward these activities as alternatives to pornography.

• Remind your child that you are there to offer the support they need. Always.

Living Free

You have reached the end of these pages, but this is by no means the end of your journey. Parenthood is an ongoing experience of highs and lows. Some of the most beautiful moments we share in life are those we learn from, and those that draw us closer together.

While I have hope that someday pornography will cease to be such a heavy burden on our society, I take comfort in knowing that there are things we can do to relieve ourselves of this burden in the here and now. Starting at home, we can begin to plant the seeds for greater change.

I hope you can feel the power you have within you. I hope you feel confident in sharing what you've learned with your child. While children are extremely vulnerable to the contents of Pandora's Box, with your help they can learn to reject pornography.

The purveyors of pornography are powerful and will continue to flood the earth with their disturbing and harmful material. Their goal is to get children addicted to their drug, and get them addicted young.

But never forget this. You and your child have the most powerful defense of all, and that's a loving, deep and abiding relationship, something the porn industry will never have.

My best to you!

Gail

APPENDIX

A   Two States of Mind Bubble Diagram

B   Thinking Errors vs. Barriers of Protection

C   Costs and Benefits Diagram

D   S.T.O.P. Diagram and Coloring Page

E   Action Plan (Child)

F   Action Plan (Parent)

G   Discussion Questions

Two States of Mind Bubble Diagram

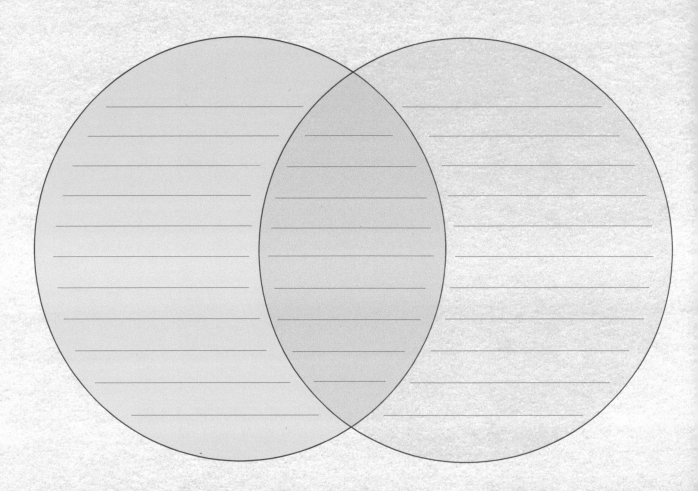

In the left circle write logical statements about your problem.

In the right circle write how you feel about it.

In the center bring your ideas together to write a plan.

Two States of Mind Bubble Diagram

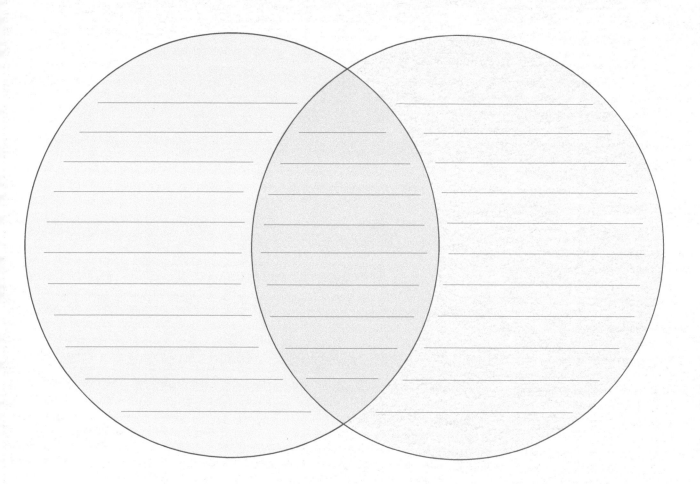

In the left circle write logical statements about your problem.

In the right circle write how you feel about it.

In the center bring your ideas together to write a plan.

Two States of Mind Bubble Diagram

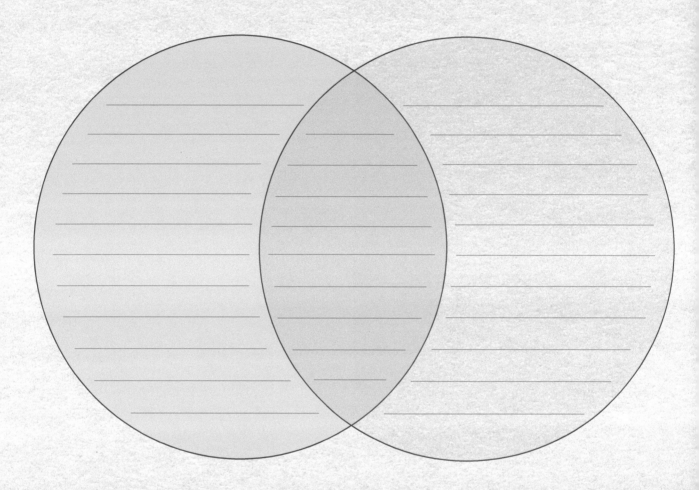

In the left circle write logical statements about your problem.

In the right circle write how you feel about it.

In the center bring your ideas together to write a plan.

Two States of Mind Bubble Diagram

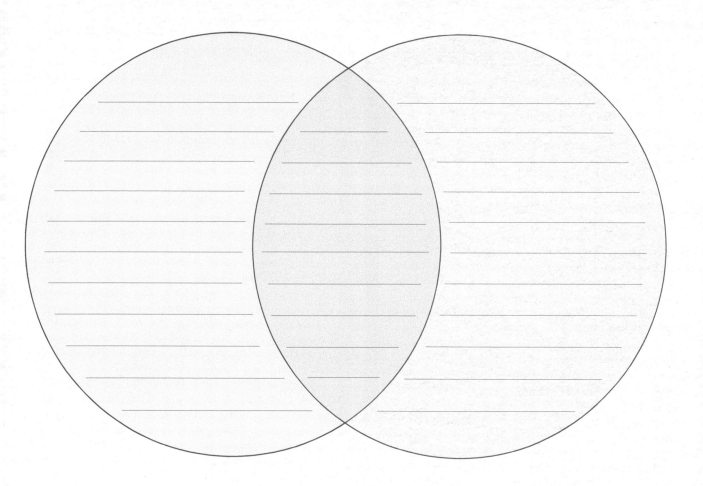

In the left circle write logical statements about your problem.

In the right circle write how you feel about it.

In the center bring your ideas together to write a plan.

Thinking Errors vs. Barriers that Protect

Thinking Errors

Barriers that Protect

Thinking Errors vs. Barriers that Protect

Thinking Errors

Barriers that Protect

Costs and Benefits

Costs

Benefits

Costs and Benefits

Costs

Benefits

STOP

STOP

THINK

OPEN

PROCEED

D

STOP

THINK

OPEN

PROCEED

My Action Plan (Child)

I am accessing porn on these devices

_____

_____

_____

I am accessing porn at these places & times

_____

_____

_____

To limit physical access to pornography I will

_____

_____

_____

Before I view porn I often feel

_____

_____

Here are some things I can do about those feelings

_____

_____

_____

_____

When I view porn I feel

_____

_____

_____

After I view porn I feel

_____

_____

_____

Some alternatives to pornography that also make me feel good are

_____

_____

_____

_____

I can use my logical state of mind to help me stop looking at porn by

_____

_____

_____

When I am tempted to look at porn I will take the following actions

_____

_____

I can reduce my thinking errors by reminding myself of the barriers that help protect me, such as

_____

_____

_____

I can see a stop sign in my head and know that it's there to protect me. When I see this stop sign and act accordingly I feel

_____

_____

_____

The costs of using porn are

_____

_____

_____

I want to stop viewing porn because

_____

_____

_____

My parents can help support me by

_____

_____

_____

_____

My Action Plan (Child)

I am accessing porn on these devices

_____
_____
_____

I am accessing porn at these places & times

_____
_____
_____

To limit physical access to pornography I will

_____
_____
_____

Before I view porn I often feel

_____
_____

Here are some things I can do about those feelings

_____
_____
_____
_____

When I view porn I feel

_____
_____

After I view porn I feel

_____
_____
_____

Some alternatives to pornography that also make me feel good are

_____
_____
_____
_____

I can use my logical state of mind to help me stop looking at porn by

_____
_____
_____

When I am tempted to look at porn I will take the following actions

_____
_____

I can reduce my thinking errors by reminding myself of the barriers that help protect me, such as

_____
_____

I can see a stop sign in my head and know that it's there to protect me. When I see this stop sign and act accordingly I feel

_____
_____
_____

The costs of using porn are

_____
_____
_____

I want to stop viewing porn because

_____
_____

My parents can help support me by

_____
_____
_____
_____

E

My Action Plan (Parent)

My child has access to porn on these devices
_____
_____

My child has access to porn at these places and times
_____
_____

To limit physical access to pornography I will
_____
_____

When I recognize that my child is struggling with resisting pornography
and/or struggling with appropriate coping techniques, I will
_____
_____

I will set a positive example by
_____
_____

I will encourage safe Internet usage in our home by
_____
_____

I will encourage my child to feel safe and to continue to discuss pornography use
with me by
_____
_____

The costs of using porn are
_____
_____

I want my child to stop viewing porn because
_____
_____

I will support my child by
_____
_____
_____
_____
_____
_____

My Action Plan (Parent)

My child has access to porn on these devices
_____
_____

My child has access to porn at these places and times
_____
_____

To limit physical access to pornography I will
_____
_____

When I recognize that my child is struggling with resisting pornography
and/or struggling with appropriate coping techniques, I will
_____
_____

I will set a positive example by
_____
_____

I will encourage safe Internet usage in our home by
_____
_____

I will encourage my child to feel safe and to continue to discuss pornography use
with me by
_____
_____

The costs of using porn are
_____
_____

I want my child to stop viewing porn because
_____
_____

I will support my child by
_____
_____
_____
_____
_____
_____

Pornography Discussion Script

Opener *How will you open the conversation? Remember to remain calm and stress the importance of working together. Don't forget to include your goals.*

_____

_____

Explaining Addiction *What example(s) will you use to explain the cycle of addiction to your child?*

_____

_____

Parental Checkpoint

☐ I am remaining calm and objective

☐ I have reminded my child that looking at pornography does not make them "bad"

Encouraging Your Child's Perspective *How will you invite your child to participate in the conversation? Consider some questions that will encourage them to share their thoughts and feelings about pornography and addiction.*

_____

_____

Explaining the Mind *What example(s) will you use to illustrate the Two States of Mind Model?*

_____

_____

Uniting Concepts *How will you introduce the Two States of Mind Bubble Diagram (appendix A) and encourage your child to consider how the two states of mind act in relation to pornography?*

_____

_____

Working Together *What will you say and do to show your child that you want to work together on this problem? What will you say and do to encourage your child's input into a plan to reject pornography?*

_____

_____

Pornography Discussion Script

Opener *How will you open the conversation? Remember to remain calm and stress the importance of working together. Don't forget to include your goals.*

_____

_____

Explaining Addiction *What example(s) will you use to explain the cycle of addiction to your child?*

_____

_____

Parental Checkpoint

☐ I am remaining calm and objective

☐ I have reminded my child that looking at pornography does not make them "bad"

Encouraging Your Child's Perspective *How will you invite your child to participate in the conversation? Consider some questions that will encourage them to share their thoughts and feelings about pornography and addiction.*

_____

_____

Explaining the Mind *What example(s) will you use to illustrate the Two States of Mind Model?*

_____

_____

Uniting Concepts *How will you introduce the Two States of Mind Bubble Diagram (appendix A) and encourage your child to consider how the two states of mind act in relation to pornography?*

_____

_____

Working Together *What will you say and do to show your child that you want to work together on this problem? What will you say and do to encourage your child's input into a plan to reject pornography?*

_____

_____

CPSIA information can be obtained
at www.ICGtesting.com
Printed in the USA
LVHW07n1555010818
585594LV00009B/136/P